Brain soup: a collection of poems

Chayla Sherman

BookLeaf Publishing

Presentation by *BookLeaf Publishing*

Web: www.bookleafpub.com

E-mail: info@bookleafpub.com

ISBN: 9789357210713

First edition 2022

DEDICATION

Dedicated to my friends and family, without you, I would not have made it here, your presence is my most cherished gift.

Thank you to ever soul I've met, and those I've yet to meet. You continue to inspire me and propel my imagination forward.

ACKNOWLEDGEMENT

I'd like to acknowledge all the people who kept pushing me forward despite insecurities telling me to quit.

So thank you, for the listening ears, and words of confidence. Thank you for the gentle corrections and advice.

Thank you for late night pep talks and hugs and tears.

You all are so special and I am lucky I’ve gotten the chance to know you.

And thank you, dear reader, and for giving give my words a chance. I hope they speak to you and inspire. You are enough and you aren't alone. I love you.

PREFACE

This collection of poems was part of a 21 day challenge for novice writers to push their creativity. A poem required to be turned in at the end of each day. At the end of the challenge the poems are published.

Hold, Please

Hold please
I cannot remember
Who I am

Only

Who I am not

I am not the smart girl
I am not the thin girl
I am not bold
or forward

I am not brave
I am not graceful
Or clever

I am not the one who got away
nor am I the family pride and joy

I am not successful
Or punctual
Or organized

I am not the first one picked
Nor am I the one remembered

Who am I?

There's no memory that I hold
Where I got to decide
Who I am

I have been a service
A listener

A lover
A substitution
Someone disposable
And a burden

I have been eager
To give all of me
For crumbs
Give every piece of me
Just to feel like
I belong
That I am worthy of love

Please hold
for I am still deciding
What to do with
A shell of potential
Laid to rest at my feet

I decide to pick
And choose
Who I am to be
With careful deliberation

I am on a journey
Of discovery
To grieve loss
And celebrate birth
To appreciate all the wonder
This life has to offer

Who am I ?

I am kind
And funny
I am full of love
free to any who choose to accept
I am beautiful in my flaws
I am pieces stitched together
To make new out of old
To grow and thrive
And break cycles

I am choosing to nurture
The parts of me forgotten
Abandoned
Lost

Shunned
Every bit of me
That was too much for you

Hold please
Because I am learning
To breathe for the first time
I am learning to love the one thing
I have hated my whole life
I am learning there is more to me
Then the empty placed at my feet

For at my feet
Hallow ground lies
Should I choose to embrace
What is beneath the surface
Where seeds lie dormant
Just waiting
For the right season
To bloom

Of You

Of you

When I think of you:

We are Sleeping in on a Sunday morning,
Tangled limbs in fluffy blankets,
Dust motes dancing in sunbeams.

When I'm lost in the kitchen,
Your embrace is heady and hungry,
Getting flour on your favorite shirt.

You twirl me and sway,
To James Taylor,
Letting the pancakes burn.

Oh how

When your fingers brush my thighs,
you always breathe me in,
Just before you kiss my neck.

I fantasize about those fingers,
The gentle whisper of a touch,
When you stroke my cheek.

Tender gazes under your lashes,
Butterfly kisses,
Leaving me breathless.

If only

We could get in a car,
With no destination,
Just old music and each other.

I'd hold your hand,
You'd Steal glances of me,
When you think I'm not watching.

Drive until the sun goes down,
So we can lay in the backseat,
And the stars watch us kiss.

At Sea

Words tumble and toss
Like waves in my mouth
Lapping at my tongue
As the tide comes in

My brain fills
With tide pools
Full of the remnants of sentences
Unspoken
Or memories that storm in
Causing riptides
Pulling me out to sea

The words wash over me
Over my tongue
As it traces each syllable
Against my teeth

I dare not speak them
For once the current takes hold
I cannot stop what is washed ashore
So tread water as I may

I paddle

But sometimes on a sunny day
I am able to float
To embrace the weather
bask in the sun and gentle water

But even on those sunny days
Deep under the surface
Thoughts rush through
In the undertow
Pulling and pushing

Despite it all I am here
Weather worn and tired
But I keep my eyes on the horizon
For life is too beautiful to escape

Demons

There's demons
That have waged war
On my heart and soul
Infecting my brain
Leaving scars on my body and perception

Demons who held me in possession
With no angel on my shoulder
I fought a war
Against myself for myself
A serpent attacking its own tail

I won
But not without losing
I claimed victory of nothing
For all was lost
No man's land is where I lay home

Born again to fight again
Mother and child all the same
The healer and the protector
The hurt and defenseless

All one in the same

Is there middle ground to wave my white flag
Or am I a prisoner of war
Can I get both sides to agree to disagree
Time is running out
And I am spread thin
How much shadow work
Does it take?

Will there ever be peace?
A day when I
Won't look over my shoulder
And jump
At every loud noise
A day I can finally
Be free

My Body

This body is a miracle
It is a miracle I've kept her here
I have treated her like shit
I have marred her skin
Starved her body
Assaulted with my words and actions
Allowing others to do the same
To use her and belittle

She deserves to be celebrated
She has kept me safe
Protected me
She bore my children
She is so strong
All she's been through, she persists
I don't deserve you
Yet she loves me, still

I am so very grateful
You have given everything
Every scar and blemish and wrinkle
The stretch marks

The ounces and pounds
Every one
A miracle
To show that I’m alive

Thank you for loving me
Even when no one else has
Thank you for keeping me safe
I have the opportunity
To try again
I’m not wasting any more time
Thank you
For another chance
To love you

Soul Food

If I could

I would feed the masses
Any broken heart
Or empty belly
I would fill with fresh bread
and soup

I would pour my love into a bowl
Mix in compassion and
Understanding
I would cook with intention
And nurture you back to health

If I could heal every ailment
I would
With my ears and a spoon
I could change the world

Draw in kindred spirits
With laughter

And the promise of
Flavor
A full belly
And a place to rest
Your bones

Eat from my table
You're always welcome
I can always make
Something out of nothing
To share
My mother taught me
Not even enemies
Deserve to go hungry

I'll be waiting
Come when you can
I'll leave the kettle
On the stove

Rainy Day

Skin presses on cold glass
On a drizzly autumn day
In comfy mismatched socks
Tea in one hand
The other threaded in your curls

You lay in my lap
Reading poetry between my thighs
One hand griping the book
The other
 My soul

Your steady voice
Vibrates up my spine
Warm words tickle my skin
Sonnets deep
With promises of
A "love that was more than love"

I watch your lashes flutter
As you scan each word
Your lips and tongue dance
In swift fluid stokes

To bring words to life

I can only hope
When my turn comes
My tongue matches
In grace
And enthusiasm

I press my lips to yours
Soft and surprised
You greet me eagerly
Laughter bubbling
up your throat
Into me
You smile into my kiss
Cupping my cheek
You look at me

When you resume
I sip my tea
And stroke your hair once more
As you recite for me
Every profound word
For there is no place I'd rather be
Then here
With you

Brainworm

Brain worm
I can't stop the chewing
He's nibbled in
And out
My brain is threadbare
From his banquet

I am not sure what I'm trying to remember

But it feel so crucial
Little flickers
Like homespun movies
When I blink my eyes
If it's too quiet
They echo

I feel like if I reach out far enough
I'd be able to grasp it
Just lean a little further
But the further I go
The deeper I plunge

Into insanity

But it feels welcome here
I am home here
Where thoughts crash
And there's a song somewhere
Stuck on repeat
What was it
I was going to say?
'Spose it doesn't matter anyway

Trust the process
Everything is gonna be ok
Perhaps it's better
To figure out who I am
If I can't remember who I was

Forever Home

A modest home
Just big enough for us
Where we can sink roots
To make our own

We'll decorate every holiday
Memories live in the walls
Laughter echoes in
The foundation
There's always food
filled with magic
Music crooning softly

No more turning in the keys
No more pit stops
A place where our door
Can be open
Gardens full of love
Room to watch
my babies grow
A place to age

And pass down

Somewhere safe
Where hands don't hurt
And words are kind
Where secrets
Aren’t boxes packed in the attic
Hidden
So the neighbors don’t see

My home will be cozy
And quaint
Where my children
Know they are loved
And respected
And appreciated
They will be accepted
No matter who they bring home
Or crazy new thing
They’ve just got to try

Help Wanted

I have a spot in my heart
Maybe you could fill it
I heard you're like me
Are you lonely?
Or just in need of company?

Let's walk with no destination
I will listen to you talk
About nothing
And everything all at once

Explore with me
With child-like glee
Museums and places
I've never been
Study me
While I learn you

I want to count
The creases on your hands
Memorize the texture of your skin
Let me read you like a book

And tell you my favorite part

I will treat the pages with reverence
As long as you promise
To lick your fingers
Before turning my pages
Breathe in my scent
And hold me close

Drink me in
Like your favorite cup of coffee
Devour me whole
I promise to be sweet
Like chocolate cake

I have nothing but mischief planned
So run with me
And laugh with me
Because I can think of nothing better
Then your head back
With laughter
Like music made only for me
I'd do anything
To hear it

Afternoons filled with free time
To lounge in each other's arms
To tickle
Until you squirm
To look in your eyes
When you look
Down at me
Electricity crackling
Right before
You kiss me breathless
It will never be enough
Until
You consume my soul

Untitled

Sometimes I wonder if
God had an issue
With who I was before
For all the trials of this life
Have left a turbulent shake
On the fragile frame of reality I've constructed

But then I remember
I am more than a lesson
I am more than karmic debt

I am made of stardust
And love
And whimsy
I laugh
and fuck
and feel
I am humanity

Every breath is stronger than the last
I made it through this life
I have scars

and bags
and wrinkles

I have learned so much
In such a short time
And I am so thankful
For every person who told me I couldn't
For everyone who said
"You're not enough"
"You'll never make it"

I am thankful for every hardship
And heartbreak
And trial
In this life

I am me because of it
I wouldn't change anything
I will not stand ashamed
Of what I've endured
To become me

Motherhood made me

Motherhood made me tired
I'm always so tired
Running on e
Love bucket dry
Touch and tapped out

Motherhood made me anxious
Paranoid of everything
Everyone a threat
Living so dangerously
Cycles my head

Motherhood made me open my eyes
How couldn't I see
What was in front of me
How did I not know how broken I was
Healing my inner child
Was just one tiny step
In this shit show I present as myself

Motherhood made me grow up
To reflect outside myself

To always see every perspective
To humble myself because
We're all so fucking weird
And frail
And human

Motherhood made me change
My thoughts are constantly spinning
Reflecting
Critiquing
Begging me to do better next time
Choosing to break cycles
And love them endlessly

Motherhood made me strong
Advocating for them
Even when everyone told me I was wrong
Delusional or even jaded
Fighting past every obstacle
So they can have the best life I can provide

Motherhood made me laugh
I enjoy the little things
The tender moments I can hold in my heart
Locked away just for us
Tickle fights and silly faces

And movie nights packed in close

Motherhood made me cherish
Every memory
Because I'm running out of time
To give them the best
And that's all I want
Is to see them succeed
No matter what it takes

Fire spirits

I watch the flames dance
Flicker and twirl
Beckon me
With delicious warmth
That only a they could produce

I am intoxicated
On the crackle
And glitter
of the burning wood
My sweet Ember
I am mesmerized

Captivated by the glow
There is nothing but
This moment
My eyes flick with the choreography

Whispers
Of the wood
Murmurs of sweet nothings
At the kiss of the flame

The crackle and sigh
Flames lick and lap
Consuming

Even in death
There is so much beauty
You still give your all
While sputtering out
In a soft bed of ash
I still love you so
And wait for your rebirth
Like a phoenix from flame

I know you will always greet me
On the coldest of nights
As long as I summon you
I will have the joy of faeries
Dancing in my hearth

Self Taught

Every fiber of my being
I constructed
Out of nothing

Over the years
I have learned
To mend my own wounds
After being pulled apart
Thread by threat

Everything I am
Is self-taught
I built myself
Toe to nose tip
I am still flawed
Uneven
A work - in - progress

I exist
And I am stretching my limbs
Testing endurance
Yearning to thrive

After so long dying

Accepting myself
Despite the fact
My body is soft and dimpled
Gravity isn't my friend
In any sense
And awkward in every way

I am beautiful in all my imperfections
A home cooked meal
I am worthy of love and joy
Even if someone doesn't like
Home cooked meals

Let's live

There's still so much
I haven't experienced
Movies I haven't seen
Places I've never been
Music I've never heard
Art I haven't made

And I feel the looming pressure
That time is running out
I hear the clock ticking
Feel the weight
Of the cold heavy steel
Every moment heavier
Then the last

All these things I have yet to do
With my children
The days are disappearing
Faster than I can keep up
Where are my babies?

The years are passing

Just a little too quickly
How do I slow this down?
I need to call tech support
Maybe ctrl - alt - delete

If this is all that's left
I refuse
To deny my children
All the beauty
This world holds in
People
Experiences
Flavors

I will live
So they are not afraid
Of landing
When they spread their wings

Dark Days

Some times the darkness creeps
Shadows slip under my pillow
And slither in while I sleep
Making nests
Infiltrating my brain

I wake not know why I feel off
Mornings are too loud
The day rolls on
With hidden spikes

Booby traps lie in wait
Lurking
Until opportunity arrives
And SNAP
I'm caught in the muck

Help
I'm being invaded
Demons pluck my heartstrings
And take over my emotions

I feel like my body's turning
Inside out
Silent screams and tears
Only I see
Only I feel

I am broken again
Unless I fight
But I'm so tired
Who will fight for me
Can anyone see

I am alone
With my secrets
And despair
I will fight this war
Again

Momma

Little girl
Deep inside
Are you lost?
Why do you hide?

I am here
Will you come out?
I will wipe your tears
Embrace you tenderly

No one will hurt you
You don't have to fight
Please don't hide
I promise I'm not leaving

I'm always by your side
You are me
And I am you
I will stay forever

I will listen to you

And encourage you
Give you everything
I needed

I will tame you
Feral child in my heart
With warmth
And kisses

Soon you will see
There is more than life
There is more than pain
And fear

Take my hand
I won't let go
I am your protector
I am momma now

Strong

I don't want to be strong
I'm so tired of holding it all
Someone step in
Please

Let me rest
And live
Surviving my whole life
Has left me brittle

Let me enjoy the sun
Mosey through flowers
Read books
And laugh until I'm sore

I am unraveling
My body needs mending
But if I'm the seamstress
My hands are occupied

Even still

I hold it together
I give of myself
Even when the cup is empty

I want to sleep
Let someone bring me coffee
To heal
and wake up better

But strong I must be
I have little eyes
And hearts
To protect and love

If it means they will live
I will be strong
I will power though it all
Ease the burden of living

Give it all to me
If that means they will thrive
They deserve a childhood
They don't have to recover from

I will give them the softness
The love and tenderness
I will make a difference
No matter what it takes

My Children

I see myself
In each one of you
In odd little angles
And dancing light
You are my children
And I am so full
My heart brims over
My throat chokes
And my eyes fill with tears

You all are so beautiful
In your silly messy ways
You inspire me daily
To change
Be better
To love unconditionally
With no expectations

You deserve the world
I wish I could give it to you
I'd do anything
To make the world more gentle
Accepting

To allow you to stay little
and goofy
Where you could be yourself

I never want any of you
To give in or fold
Be you
Unapologetically
Stand firm
And never lose sight
Of who you really are

You are my children
And you can do anything
Be anything
I will hold your hand
Brace you through it all
Pick you up and carry you
If that's what it takes
For you to succeed
I love you
Forever and always

Wanderlust

There's a yearning
In my soul
An unknown entity
Calls to me
Knows me
In a way that is primal
My gut reacts
On instinct
Lurching in the direction
My soul calls home

I often feel I am spinning
Pulled in circles
By this being
Who calls me home
I wish I could describe
How incredibly lost
I am
No sense of direction
To aide in my journey

Adventure lies in wait
Quests to take me

Deeper into the unknown
Just listening to the empty
For a whisper
Acknowledging I'm on my way

Hotter or colder
Like childhood games
I'm enticed by the magic promised
Snippets of home
Play in softly woven dreams
So close
I could almost reach out
And hold it in my palms

My soul aches
For something I've not seen
In this lifetime
If I could grasp an image
I might know where to search
I wouldn't feel so alone
Maybe I have family waiting
I don't want to keep them
I must be on my way

Brain Soup

They say soup is for the soul
But where does the soup
come from?
What concoction
Of delicious morsels
Is worthy of quenching
The soul

I could offer broth of riches
Oh yes
Priceless jewels
Exotic spices
Status
And power
All worthless in the eyes
of the soul

I've searched the universe
In all it's glory
To find a soup to sate
This wild hunger
And mighty is the meager
For the soup is

In ourselves
This fragile meat suit
Houses our chef

They are the humble servant
Holding together
Our flesh and spirit
A faithful friend
Spooning bite after slurp
Of brain soup
Into our souls

Our brain
Is all things
They hold every
Beautiful creation
To be sang
Or read
Or painted
Every thing in existence
And all that have yet to become
Started here

www.ingramcontent.com/pod-product-compliance
Lightning Source LLC
Chambersburg PA
CBHW051737130826
49812CB00033B/897
* 9 7 8 9 3 5 7 2 1 0 7 1 3 *